Ping-Pong In The Rain

Knotbrook Taylor

For Elana
love Knotbrook x

erbacce-press
Liverpool UK

Acknowledgements:

My thanks go to the editors of the following publications: Northwords Now, Horizon Review, One–Eyed jacks. I would also like to thank John Glenday for his support and encouragement with the V poems and Jo Bell and all the people on the Facebook Group 52 (circa2014) for their feedback and encouraging words.

erbacce-press publications Liverpool UK 2014

erbacce-press.com
ISBN: 978-1-907878-68-8

For Edith

Contents:

Versus

(poems of random junction)

Cape Cod V thanatos

(with its cranberry bogs and crystal clear lakes…)

   curling, curling, curling smoke: smoke: curling smoke: curling
   the old man's friend…

   thanatos is that a Greek island?

(with its clapboard houses and empty beaches…)

   they-groups: out-groups: we all belong in one.

   if it was an island it wouldn't be much fun
   cocktail hour would be mine's a tomato juice
   the beaches really would be empty: though tomb-stoning might catch
   on or self harm (after midnight): outcome - outpatient

(why not go whale watching or just kick back…)

   there would be in-groups for gate crashers and car crashers
   ejaculatio praecox on their tee-shirts: knives in their backs

(just minutes from dining, shopping, sailing)

   Gorecki's third would be top of the charts: my father would have loved it
   he could sing his song – all the days are cold and weary – over and over

      smoke: smoke: curling: curling

the equation of edge V photographing Uranus

she said Vernon had lost his *edge* but that Michael still had his

we asked *what is edge?*

let me put it in a mathematical way she said…

size + frequency + charisma + looks + X = edge

what is X we shouted (we were affronted now)(feeling rather inadequate)?

and what about creativity? what about danger?

and humour? (and steadfastness…)

X is that indefinable quality that some men have

creativity is in….she said after some thought (thank God said the writers)

oh and humour too

and sensitivity…maybe

in the corner of the drunken room the sky at night was showing on the TV: someone was interviewing a man who took pictures of the planets with a converted telescope in his back garden.

In response to some missed question he said…

Photographing Uranus can be difficult on a cloudy night…

so we said *in summary what you're saying is..*

size + frequency + charisma + looks + humour + sensitivity + X = edge

the room fell silent – the nature of the planets in the Solar System continued to amaze and a question hung in the air

– that we were too afraid to ask…

old ladies V the future of money

they smile and joke and shuffle unsteadily
but basically you know where you are with an old lady

banks crashing like big trucks into the sides
of their own office skyscrapers

all very sub-prime crime and grime – nominal – notional
the futures boys shafting everyone – including themselves

the oil is going – China is coming – India is coming
make way – the cake on my plate is mine – if I finish it mummy will die

some old ladies are secretly very rich and careful with their liquidity
quiddity – quiddity – cupidity – (cupidity is not about arrows)

let them regulate world banking – they can give us 50p 50c to buy lunch
no-one will go hungry – no-one will go greedy – some respect will be
shown

lets shuffle into the future on careful feet – in slippers – to stop us
slipping
flipping – ripping the guts out of it all

let them ease into economic bliss
pleased with their own quantitative easing

...one for you...one for you...one for you

...and no fighting... the lot of you!

PJ Harvey V ping-pong in the rain

dwarfed by the jaws of the new hospital
an incongruous green table

if a crow were made human
it would look like Polly

the white page! the white page!

rocking back slowly
melting into the shadow at the back of the stage
in a leather corset
with a zither strapped to her chest

strumming the white page
a witch in black – or an angel

(I don't want her to die but)

(I don't want her to get better)

I want to stroke those sleek black feathers

(as I stroke your wasted arm)

look up at that beak – I see the death of which you sing

when we were folded in the shadows – beyond all clinical light
she told me
about the white page

outside the hospital
two small boys play ping-pong
in the rain…

owl V lift

white noise of leaves: night waits for a scream
      (yours or mine?)
in the eyes of an owl
broken eggs make a fine and bloody mosaic

overseer of midnight
(*soul of the recently dead: some say*)

        if you press and keep pressed
        the *close door* button
        select your floor
        your lift will go there without interruption

I have no knowledge of this bird
other than once on my balcony
a sentient meeting
silence flown
its weird logic lost in the scrub

        I make the long walk to your ward
        my eyes marbles
        I have no wisdom here
        slow - slower - I - go

ABBA V I'm gonna die one day

lets all go to the races - she said
there's horses and an ABBA tribute band
we could take champagne and borrow Belinda's 4x4
I could wear my white suit – we could all wear white!

>
> less and less now
> I wake in the middle of the night and
> suddenly with a kersmack! – a dead cert!
>
> ## *one – day – I - won't - be*

does it mean I'm not so scared to die?
does it mean I don't want to even think about dying?
does it mean I'm gonna go and see an ABBA tribute band?
with a dancing queen in a white suit?

yes

and

no!

> I have put a stipulation in my will

(*can you hear the drums Fernando?* – yes I can every day – can't you?)

> about the funeral…

no whites shall be worn!

beetroot V whirlwind

the seed of a beetroot is not red
it is tiny – insignificant
but put in the earth and fed - it grows
its root swells and bulges like a fat man's belly
to become - in high summer
a vibrant blood-red-entity
which can stain and sustain

when a whirlwind comes to town
you will know about it
destruction is legion
cars - picked and dashed
house roof ripped
and our bedrooms rudely exposed

later: dead fish on the lawn
someone else's underwear
hanging from the monkey puzzle
and a blessed
but somehow terrifying
silence

of the two phenomena…

…love is a beetroot!

black spirals V kiss parties

when I kiss you it all becomes still
all my personalities have joined hands in a circle
suddenly they have stopped wringing

if you dowse you will find them
your twigs will fly around the room
in ever decreasing loops – then
 your hands will feel dead
said the spooky-man

fucking black spirals!

I kiss you - we are talking – we are learning
you said you went to kissing parties when you were a girl
now we have our own - *party for two*

standing stones
an abandoned quarry
a fault line
underground streams and fractures
rocks: shit we can't even see
radiation: ley lines…

…the colour of the spirals
  we can change them!

(apparently)…

the lady of the forest V the butt plug

a butt plug can be a comfort

the lady of the forest is a mystery

both are strange - both can be painful

pray for us…….

panic on the cliff V mummification

I want a carapace: a shell: to be isolated from the world
so wrap me in polythene and bring me back into myself
I want to be insulated: bundled up
focussed: helpless: safe
body present – mind cut adrift on a sweated sensual sea
wrap me and rescue me…

memory is the coal we burn to live – everything is not rotten

some of the birds who live on the cliff can only fly by falling into the air

we refute Muldoon's black rainbow…

      the jumper stood on the cliff and said:
      I'm not afraid of change I'm afraid of staying the same…

      and when he jumped – there was no last second panic in his eye
      just peace – he really knew how to have a good

      (if exceptionally brief)

      time…

programmed cell death V parking the car

apoptosis: damn right: its enough to make you…
when the programme screams - *abandon all cars!*

I can't think about that because there's someone in my space
and every day new bird-shit: and all the time tick-ticky

what would TOOticky say? *play the wooden flute?*: I think not
don't invest in futures: let his tyres down: slash 'em: burn it

smear Vaseline on the windscreen: he'll think its fog!
sprinkle washing powder: snow: he'll get his shovel!
but he won't get the message: doesn't stop to listen

abandon all cells…

walk to work (on a vitamin enriched egg).

rock dust V blue food

there's a thousand years of ice just up the road: so ordered by Gaia
(there's method there)

you see it's the glaciers: crushing: grinding!

spouts like an evangelist: a seer: bit of a bastard really
would dump you in a ditch if it progressed the word
coz he's got his giant apples and mighty tomatoes

carrots like truncheons

he wanders our de-mineralised-interglacial-hinterland
bemoaning its ugliness

these rolling hills should be covered in trees!
where is the green baize?

all we need is rock dust: from volcanoes: he added later

he's lucky: he's angry: he's righteous: (he doesn't wash)

and conveniently ignored the deer and the sheep - who eat all the trees

blue cheese, (the rare) blue trout, blueberries

(mercy: I was going to start a trend…)

R.S.I. V clouds

tap dancing again: too much
clickety-click: all the day: I write: what you say
until it hurts: until I spasm: in the finger muscles

clouds form faces through the window
they whisper: too quiet
mountains above the mountains
they shout: silence
they are the power: the exemplar
we must change: we can slowly become
God is a cloud

clicky-clicky-plastic-clicky-rat-at-tata-ta-ta-ta-ta…

this overriding general symptom
is not a…
righteous overriding general symptom

there's a little red plane appearing between cumulus
its pulling a message

freedom is expensive!

this server is corrupt: save
all servers will become corrupt: save

you are a corrupter of data
all corruption is data: translate: too late

warning if you feel pain while using this equipment
seek advice from a medical practitioner

doctor doctor: I keep going back…

burying beetle V undertakers

I was built for this purpose: burying the dead

my granny used to say as the lord makes them
the lord pairs them
there always two of us

dead mice can walk again
though dead rabbits can only shrug and snuggle down
bears eventually stop twitching

you have to be quiet: respectful
slow and in black
if you think they have been murdered you will be mistaken
they were just trying to reach the bathroom

we use the meat to feed our babies: can even preserve it
it's a working marriage: under the ground

one day they will lay the corpses out in a field
by morning they will be gone
all we'll have to do is provide the Daimler

self V *self*

in Bladerunner
at the end…
      (near the end!) (Soren said - *if you are happy: this is despair!*)

…when the replicant dies
and the rain drips…
      (*if you are sad*) (*obviously*) (*this too, is despair!*)

…down his face
and as the dove…
      (spirit) (do robots have a spirit?) (do I?)

…rises above the city
I cry
      (I (we) rehearse!)

(finitude)   beans on toast and crosswords…

(infinitude)   when I imagine *attack ships on fire off the shoulder of Orion*

      (beyond what he says: please check out Rutger's facial expressions too….)

Buzzard V Napoli

out on the road today
a buzzard in a tree
and a daydream of Naples

(Day 1. fumaroles and grappa)

rocks with mortal indecision – back and forth
unsure of what it is I mean
ready to fly but only if he has to

(Day 3. Castle Elmo - saw Escher and Velasquez)

the leaves seethe - his old wings ache
in a warm unseasonal breeze

(Cumae) (Vesuvius) (prego!)

what is it I see
in his side on eye

(hesitation)

it'll be the death of him
he knows and holds it
sure as thunder and road-kill

(Day 6. Herculaneum: children with accordions
begging on the train)

disseminated primatemaia V Alzheimer's

(Gaia is suffering from a plague of people: Lovelock)

seven out of ten for sadness: is what she gave to remembering her
father's funeral it used to be a ten but the memory changes each time she
recalls it…

he once told her: *there's a lot of love around you:* he never was a mystic

now her mother is being eaten from the inside out: *like Dutch Elm
disease* (said her quack) decisions are impossible: *I just have to….: is that me
in the picture…: old fossil* this gets an eight: the machine is wearing out:
memories are being deleted (bit by bit)

6 billion people (and still rising): a collective memory bank: trillions of
precious moments its like travelling back in time to: Niagara Falls:
catching that spider crab: her first bottle of Bud…

*imagine each one of us losing their memories: wandering the cities and
towns: bumping into abandoned cars: trying to get back a feeling: a
word: humankind in its own era of solitude: everything we have learned:
all connection to the planet lost…*

they gave him the doom drug to slow down his heart: *it replicates the
hormones released by the body before we die:* (he said)

the room was closing in and there was more pressure in the air…

did you see a tunnel with a light?

crow trap V dementia care

cries repeatedly
cocks a beady eye

love is passing between us
I like to think

hops back and forth
lucid some of the time

go insane
if you put them in a cage

emotional memory remains intact
do you touch her?

pulls hat down close
tilts bloody beak

are you afraid?

head in a bag V the dawn chorus

two little girls (they had to be ginger)(and if they weren't they are now):
this beautiful Scottish beach…(ha!)
a sunlit day: playing in the sand: they found a head in a bag: later a hand
(two hands)

up came the circus with their dishes and their questions: nice young men
speaking to cameras: (*nothing like this ever happens here!*) (*what about
the Polish guy that was murdered last year!*) out came the Peelers with
their rakes and clue detection: we love the macabre: beats government
taxes: *I wonder if they did it with saws or axes*

two days later they called for a diver: he jumped in the harbour and
found a mystery suitcase (had to be opened in lab conditions): it was
the rest of her…

turns out she was from Lithuania (*oh they're used to murder in
Transylvania* said Jimmy's dad while we watched the Grand
National)(*oh those girls how will they ever grow up unburdened*)(what
about the father in Lithuania? who's going to pay for his cancer
treatment now?): not to mention the dead woman

…in spring a hormonal message is sent to the hypothalamus of birds to
sing more at dawn: they have woken the Fates from a quiet winter: there
were blackbirds mating behind the eucalyptus: then there's the problem
with the gulls: (*noisy bastards all year round*)…

incidentally: this is not the first time body parts have washed up on
the beach round here: few years back a leg washed up: they proved it
belonged to a local trawler man: his boat had gone down in a North Sea
haboob: they had a funeral for his leg: it was very dignified: they played
Enrico Caruso on an old HMV*: even the gulls were respectful: when
the record finished, *La Somnambulist*, the needle in the grooves sounded
like the sea…

(*HMV Zonophone Horn Gramophone , circa 1911)

clarinet V automatic

(after a visit to Ardnamurchan Lighthouse)

she sits opposite him playing a clarinet
a slow haunting air

> *he used to climb the stone spiral stair*
> *to light the light an hour before dark*

her eyes never leave him
her lips delicate on the reed

> *at night each keeper was required to keep watch*
> *to ensure that the light flashed to its correct*
> *character*

the tune rises and falls
she sways from side to side

> *the roar on a stormy night*
> *was deafening*

she stops playing
and puts down the instrument

> *once lit the light begins to revolve*
> *slowly...*

spinning chair V winter banjo

I spin on my chair: the world goes round
I spin on my chair: the world comes around again

(blue-black-brown-white-blue-black-brown-white)

        In the bathing hut deep in winter
        Tooticky rolls another exotic cigarette
        lies back on a pile of warm towels
        and blows smoke rings
        into the open door of the wood stove

I like to go fast - (dopple-dopple-dopple)
a blurred and unclear world
makes me feel dizzy

as I slow down
the last few rotations
seem to go   on   and   on
I feel calm

        outside no-one much disturbs the snow
        the creeps – who are invisible
        (and also inhabit the bathing hut)
        watch as Tooticky sits up
        and begins to tune his banjo
        they smile at one-another

the spinning stops
and I wait
nothing   much   happens

later I begin to feel that old desire
I hang on as long as I can
before starting once more
to spin the chair…

the night mare V fear of intimacy

she'll come to you like an incubus: irrevocable and making an unholy racket

this is a good thing: this is your final exam

books-on-the-shelf-the-romantic-poets-keep-pressing-me-while-they-sip—sip-laudanum-sip

the god of the gaps is here

the gap is here: nothing exists beyond

and the sweat: *holy heat Batman!*

no-I-haven't-yes-I-have-no-dream-of-a-smile-a-smile-a-k-k-kiss

she'll lie on top of you and either you'll suffocate or...

I couldn't look into her eyes: I couldn't say those words: I couldn't give in

(wouldn't: you faker)

I know you are afraid: but it's a privilege son: lick her salty skin: repay your debt: say it...

(oh and do*n't let the unholy racket put you off*)

the backless dress V tiramisu

she clutches a bottle of champagne like a deb: really she's a
Debbie is it the backless dress or the back?

spine valley!: go wild in the country

used to go and stand in the rushing water: don't go there now...
...didn't want to be...: don't want to be...: am though...

tiramisu!: *where are you?* so much: in little plastic cups
their mothers have spent hours preparing: substitutes: substitution:
eggs: (s)cream

camera phones and tequila shots
in the dancing light of the mirror-ball: they enact

I think the backless dress (not the back) will outlive us all.

the wicked prince V the roadside bomb

my creation machine is finally complete: it won't be her but…
all I need is one tiny hair: so I can extract the DNA
I'll search the bath with some tweezers…

its easy… dial the number you have been given… and press enter…

ah! here we are a dainty curly one: high and dry
the water has seeped away: I am an empty bath :an oxbow

whispered the wicked prince bending to his find

I need a muse: a warm one

here's a camera… for propaganda…

in the oxbow all kinds of strange flowers bloom
like the milfoil and the bog-wort: but they are cut off: their season is short

insert the hair like so and press the button…ha ha ha

humvee: boom! no humvee

nudists on a trampoline V humanity rose

woah - umph - eeeh - ahh - no - please - boing - ooh - no - wump - boing
look away look away the skinny jumpers have come: defying gravity:
being free in the air jumping: jumping: burning their rumps on the bed
as they bounce

> Its not winking at you from the trampoline. You buy it at a garden centre on a sunny day: on a scale of 1 to 3 it has a 2 for smell. Good people plant them with small ceremonies. Say a few words of remembrance or hope. Gather their friends around quiet and respectful. Then they get a red watering can from a rusty wheelbarrow.

Its not something one might choose to see but it draws your eye.
A trampoline is a stage. Trampolines cure depression.

> (The nudists have known this for a while.)

*meanwhile; although the day is warm; here in the trees its cool
and there's a persistent smell: not of roses: but of decay: as though
something is dead and rotting: something hidden in the undergrowth:
I don't know where it comes from but every time I visit
there it is...*

tomb of the eagles V the tomb of the easy chair
(Orkney)

the wind and rain of 5000 years
let them lie until a farmer disturbed their sleep
the bones of men and the bones of eagles

the bones of men and otters
the bones of men and songbirds
in other unhidden places

passing unknown objects around the fire
holding them in order to speak
holding a fetish up to the light – perhaps it made them feel

press a button at the flickering light
see it change lean back – feel nothing

tomb of the snakes
tomb of the bulls
tomb of the dolphin

tomb of the plastic bottle
tomb of the AK47
tomb of the mortgage plan

It's a ceremonial object they bluster
(when they have no fucking idea)

used in their rituals – when their gods had to be appeased
it held magical properties

    tomb of the air conditioning system
    tomb of the road-side bomb
    tomb of the hybrid bicycle

the skull shows deformation – she must have had headaches
but good teeth and long lived

    tomb of the long lived
    tomb of the good teeth
    tomb of the pseudo religious experience

they had drawn out heads and faces like angels
running water: fire: beautiful buttons
and after death – divesting the bones of flesh
they waited to make (for reasons unknown)
an ossuary for the lost with a handful of talons

    tomb of the humanist funeral
    tomb of the flip-flop
    tomb of the easy chair

turquoise eyes V poetry

dreamed a girl with pale thighs
her turquoise eyes
telling lies

a police woman once told me
when they pull a body from the sea
it always has turquoise eyes

they say you should never use the word turquoise in a poem
but how can I not
it would disrespect the dead

and I was thinking
no matter how hard you try underwater
to keep them closed
in the end you wouldn't be able to help yourself...

weeping as a strategy V the dead whale

what if I used weeping as a strategy
would you know where you were with me?

you've been there now for two springs two summers one autumn and
a winter above the tide line – radio said you were a baby but
now you are a whale shaped mattress
you were higher off the ground when you first appeared
with some dumb trawler's hawser wrapped around your fin

I could be crying and you wouldn't know if I meant it
you should comfort me – instinctively you will
but are you being manip-ulated?

you stink and have been hanging around too long – reminding us of
what you werebig and beautiful – with it all to come – a clear blue world
the Council wanted to put a bomb under you but they can't scale the cliff
I think out there - your mummy misses you…

I say - when the whale weeps - its for real
though in all that salt water…

weltschmerz V miraculous

trains: getting out of an empty bed

the sour smell of piss: too noisy

smoking tongue: too cold

trucks never sleep: or hurt: I do

I remember a bridge: warm air moving

a torso twisting slowly: unseeing eyes

never existed: or: not existing

in Fatima: Our Lady smiles beatifically

inside they dance: outside it seems they are restless

I want to paint pictures: faux galleries: for all of eternity

I   don't   have   weeks…

Selected Poems 1996 - 2014

Invitation to Rain

it's a ghost world
a drowned postcard

the river disobeys convention: time distends
water trickles down my neck

another squall wraps around my back
my father said: *you can't escape reality*

an otter pops up: how can he swim in that spate
too late: gone under

trees wade out from the bank
dipping branches in and out

a strange fungus: a bloated sepia rose
opens on a log

a dipper sits inches from death
on a wet stone

water shears through the dam
with juggernaut abandon

talking would be impossible
if there was anyone else at the party

Lifeline

man comes into a room
room does not change

flowers in vase
continue to expire

man sits in brown chair
Swedish: velvet: art deco

man breathes
his heart beats automatically

fingers knit
here is a church; here's the steeple

opens a door of cracks and pores
church is empty

a blink; no more
man stares at his palm

his lifeline
mourns congregation

flowers overflow
what is left of their love

man exits
room disappears.

An Argument for Sculpture Parks

(viva Birmingham!)

did you think we'd hear the sea in your Zen garden?
here in the mid-lands: did you just want to fuck with our heads?

in the new renaissance we shall be art: our own installations!

those conical people: that iron man: looking: leaning
the floosie in the jacuzzi: lording it: I'll shave my head and die in a cave
burnt to a spiral wisp by Kundalini
fuck! there are no caves here in the mid-lands

buses: beamers: tall hotels: *we are all prisoners!*
and Venus: now there's a fountain: history: Italian marble

the only people you are fighting is yourselves!

my metro-sexual girl has broken: the surge is fake

the future is monochrome (with elegant ruins)!

a salamander synth line: wandering bass: *relax and swing!*　　(Japan)
it's the only thing that keeps me sane: here in the mid-lands
the boy paddling in the water is my son

we are reaching critical mass!

now he's pissing in it: his own comedy figurine
we laugh but not because it is funny: because our stars are in conjunction
or because: the crows will one day rule: hoppity-hop: caw and

smile: life's a sculpture park　　　　(registered trademark)

Ink
(less is more)

under arm a little forever

    a black hare races to nights caress

shirt-tail-spine-rise

    begging a lick or at least

        a close conversation

with a sea-bell and porpoise

    she held high a pale arm

I kissed an inky dove there

    and look - at the ankle

inviting guardian a coiled

    and fork tongued Ophidian

from this sensuous outpost

I travel to - the badlands

    find there find a small red rose, a ranunculus,

a black eyed susan

    quest again and rise

breasts left unadorned save for the silvery trail

of my slug blind tongue

on these cryptic nights I decipher you

    your imprints

your inscrutable scarabs… pointing

    these sex-mark-semiotics…

this indelible iconography…

fire all the arrows at cupids button - this erotic herald …. of a tiny tiny death

Art Lessons

they showed us Muybridge's galloping horses
conclusive proof they said
of equine flight

and Stubbs's *lion-attacking-a-horse*
its teeth in the back of her neck
claws holding her still: eye wild in an ecstasy of pain

then they sent us to the abattoir
to draw skinless horses
understand the muscles - where the bones go

they were the artists : the skinners and butchers
brutish and detached
deconstructing life with a well-honed shiv

I couldn't stay
I couldn't be like those men

retreating to the brothel
I murder a whore
over and over
in charcoal and ink

Mainbocher Corset
(monochrome by Horst P Horst)

I was thinking of all
I was leaving behind

girl in a corset
the landscape of her back

the loosened laces
head bent forward in submission

no welts or kisses
Paris before the Nazis.

Black Iris
(painting Georgia O'Keefe)

peeling herself apart
from the centre out
Georgia

darkness and promise
blunt mystery

imaginary flower
the scent of which
persists

taste
sometimes oblivion

yes
oblivion

Mis(s)behaviour : *Pardon me Boy…*

(curiosity did not kill the cat - it made the cat live longer!)

the delicate woman sitting next to me
is reading a book
I lean casually to crib the title

the misbehaviour of markets

(sadly)
this is not a talking point

the train slowly sinks into Queen Street
she gets up and puts away her book
sir! - she says
(an American)
sir! – so polite – *can I get a train for London here?*
yes! I nearly say *mam!*
so tiny - so confident - so beautiful
striding off down the platform
black hair - black boots - Japanese roots

Chattanooga(h!) Chattanooga(h!)…

His Women
(after Edvard Munch)

The harbour wife curled in the breakwater loves a different type of
man so he leaves her to her jug and her jugs.

The barmaid in the Asgardstrand café, when he got her alone,
explained she had been hurt and did not wish to be hurt again.

The clergyman's daughter shucked her clothes for a painting
then left him half-dressed.

She who played the viola on that hot summer evening
he took her photograph but did not make an impression.

The madonna who matched him drink for drink
rose in the night from his meagre pallet.

A rather young one dared him to fuck her
but he would not do it

A phantasmagoric one who's laughter haunted his dreams
but whose buttons could not be undone.

And that other one, the first one, who left him alone when he was
just a child. he remembers her coughing: her drawn skin

try as he might he can't be rid of her.

Naming the Fox

Hendrix of the woods: left handed murderer
Maxim of the coop: Fosbury flopper of Peters and Donalds
Mickey Mouse mouse-friend.

I had you in the eye of my Heckler and Koch: one snowy Bing
but I Mother Terresa'd on you
got my Billy The Kid deliberately wrong: aimed for the Neil Armstrong
it was a complete Edmund to the hunting fraternity.

Meanwhile you were barking like Waits: ready to Jonestown
in order to save the Foxy Lady by your side
ready to General Custer to my Crazy Horse
did you do it for Auden, did you do it for Shakespeare?

But anyway, I Hamlet'd it: No! I was Ghandi and Madiba
learned more about my inner Everyman in that Warhol of time
than ever you did, you Brummel of nature,
in your whole Nottingham Forest.

Tell me, oh barnyard Bundy, do you Cheshire at the corpses
of all those little Pertelotes
do you kiss each one gently with that old adult rating
at the end of your name?

Ashes

They are not used to losing
these fine young men
in their clean white shirts

their fear of a good line
their fear of the cracks

drowned in drink and laughter
they do not hear the music
or notice the swelling clouds

why should they...

Sleeping with the Light on

But it was a crow that flew away as she walked to the Quiet Gate
its voice: the rusty hinges
its voice: her unspoken monody.

    (Decide now what it is you care about!)

By the Fountain Of Remembrance
carrying some flowers an old man withers.

    (Do you know what I have to live with? she wanted to scream)

Crows: those things made from night
the ones you see hung from fences with orange bailer twine

    (When is a crow not black?)

In her dreams they were many colours
every night a new room: a new nest
their voice: the dry leaves
their voice: stones and sticks

    (Jump away Mr Crow!: go on!: jump off the world!)

Clever birds: move to the other side of the road
when the cortege arrives
and a little boy says: *I want to go home.*

    (K*eep your ancient mouths shut: stop calling me!*)

Corvus in the family Corvidae: their black is the old black
their black is the new: they shiver in their suits of feather
for all we know, a thousand years old…

    (W*hen do we begin to open?*)

Most nights she sleeps with the light on: blonde and missionary
in the shadow-land they rise: a dark glittering cloud.

    (T*he paparazzi are leaving*)

The black limousines are leaving: they go suddenly: flying away: for now
what remains as she walks to her car: possessions: memories.

    (Their voice: your voice)
    (Their voice: dust.)

Swinging the Shit

A chance meeting with Archie
who shared something of himself
and the passing of his sister
we're a membrane away
I just held her hand
death is simple.

The boys at number 53
were throwing out some books
Craig slouched while I rifled
I got Rilke and Lorca
opened the pages
death is simple they said.

I rode my bike
it was warm for January
but the wind was against me
my heart pounded at the hill
by the church.

There was a woman in the grave yard
walking three toy dogs
she was carrying their droppings
in three plastic bags.

After dinner I remembered her
walking among the dead
whistling
while swinging the shit.

What the Old Man did

when we got there he said
look what I can do

despite the oxygen tube
and the proximity of a cardboard piss bottle

he swung himself up
over the side of the bed

and stood
in his blue St Michaels

I expected a bow
or a flourish of the hands

we were obviously
impressed

then told us he'd done 3 metres in rehab
unaided

and before we left
he flipped back into bed

his feet at right angles
he lolled grinning
like a grey whiskered seal

its good to see you so recovered we said

feeding him dead-eyed-lies
like fish from a bucket.

What she did after...

1 tried her best
2 to fit everything she was
3 supposed to do into her
4 brain or on a list
5 sometimes she forgot the list
6 and wrote a new one
7 soon the
8 whole place was
9 littered with small pieces of
10 paper containing
11 telephone numbers for her sons
12 items of food
13 plans for the boiler
14 ideas for the kitchen
15 car registrations
16 birthdates
17 bank account details
18 instructions for instructions
19 now she picks up a list and
20 does whatever it says
21 writes a Christmas card
22 phones the gas man
23 bakes a cake
24 takes all his clothes to 25...

...the Oxfam shop

Ghosts in Empty Chairs

After the fireworks were over, and the wind had started to gust, we went indoors. Some people left, others sat around the kitchen table talking, drinking and eating leftovers. My time came I hugged everyone and left. I walked through the garden - saw the bonfire was still in and felt myself drawn. I stood looking down into the glowing embers being furiously polished by, what was now, a hell of a blow.

Around the edge of the fire, in a perfect semi-circle, were empty benches and empty chairs. Still strewn with blankets and tipped glasses. Suddenly I was standing in the ruins of some ancient feast. The runaway gale. The flat-cat flames. The fleeting smell of smoke: might all have been the same. What more fitting emblem of absence than an empty chair. What more ancient link than fire. What sound older than the howling and penitent wind...

No Fjords

She told me to get into the feeling. *Una fata*, one face, *una rata* one people: it was easy. The way she wrapped her arms around the trunk of an olive tree; way too easy. Yet she was afraid, real fear, of eating sardines. Still had their guts in. Of the car that passed too slowly as we walked. Of the evil eye over the door. *I just don't like it.*
The proprietor was a pregnant woman who lit up when children visited with their families. The place had twins working there, little black dresses, alluring but you could tell they had stories. The smell of vinegar high up in the back of the nose was a comfort somehow. Bats flew in and out of the wires in control but only just. I looked out across the dark bay. A ferry was leaving. She was eating swordfish; I stuck with the chicken.

Love Letter to Sunday

this is for the hum you cannot place
this is for the teachers out of class
this is for dust angels behind the green curtain
this is for paisley patterned rain
this is for a stain in the shape of a bird
this is for a ladle lying on its side
this is for that second piece of cake
this is for the crumbs no birds will peck
this is for the dish turned into a fox
this for the coats hanging from hooks
this is for the ribcage of a new bed
this is for pillow and the coolness of silk
this is for the collarbone and shoulders
this is for rolling under then rolling over
this is for being alone together
this is for the leering and face-blind philosopher
this is for the 8 o'clock dog and cockerel
this is for the doggerel of starlings
this is for the exorcism in a good laugh
this is the for the fog drifting out of the bath
this is for the suit that stays where it is
this is for the tie a grandfather gave
this is for a chemise on the back of the door
this is for underwear left on the floor
this is for perfume familiar and strange

this is for the x…

… at the end of the page

The Misery of the Butterflies
(Kierkegaard *the lepidopterist* visits Colonsay gardens)

The ringlet he flies in circles around and around the flowers
yet rarely alights to take the nectar
overcome with existential angst it cannot bring itself to be satisfied.

The red admiral searches
but his crew are tight and lost amongst the brambles and buddleia
he radiates pure grief.
(I have seen them kamikaze the indigenous cats - in their shame.)

And this I heard from a man in Austria, at the clinic,
he said the small blues here are so often depressed they hide
under the palm fronds or the sheltering rhubarb.
Blue by name blue by nature I suppose

The brimstones here experience a living hell
you can tell by the way they quiver and veer
I've seen them down by the river drowning themselves.

The cabbage whites are so nihilistic that they lay their eggs
to kill all that is good with their ravenous caterpillars.

The commas fill in the solitude between flowers – silently
and, I must say, with a lot of conviction.
I think I love them the most.

Though the grayling is so boring he must be in despair
what with being ignored
even by the hungry swallow.

I have observed that the small tortoiseshell seeks a home
in high summer - fearful of winter coming
she can't enjoy the now – I so empathise.

And the painted ladies, their poor reputations notwithstanding
are just blown here on portentous African winds.

So I crawl among the flora with my Lepidoptera Melancholia
the misery of butterflies is so achingly beautiful
that sometimes I think: I could let my own blood.

Instead I abase myself before their beautiful agony
down here among the shrubbery
sharing my plight with these pretty patterned confederates.

Windier Days

(eco-poem)

I saw red clouds speed
          dust-bowl-dust
                    as-fire-in-the-fields

I saw an oak fully bend
              this-is-a-tree
                  lonely-for-a-forest

I heard the air sing
              long-song-long-song
                  so-oh-long…

I heard, far off, the roar of a crowd
              we-love-we-love
                  we-loved-yooo…

I felt a change come
              of-a-drifting-smoke
                  of-a-crying-jasmine

smelled foreign lands
              hotter-drier
                  funeral-pyres

brushed a strange insect
              a-new-kind-of-resident
                  with-a-feverous-needle

finally I saw
          the arable land
              scatter-itself
          `   like-its-own-ashes

Baby Lacey and the Devil

You have a little potato head and crossed bewildered eyes
are you trying to work out what's happening

mostly you sleep: you do it very well
one week old and loved already.

Lucifer was once like you
he shat, cried and was utterly helpless.

His mother said he had the face of an angel
and he grew up to be one.

I once met him in the museum
too solid to fly: seemed broken.

Said his feet hurt and he suffered *the agony of gravity.*

His beautiful bronze wings weighed heavy
but, oh boy, he could hold a conversation.

Cry little one: take to the breast
(it could be your last meal)

cling fast and remember
everyone loves you: it's a good start…

Routine Manoeuvres

(Findhorn Beach)

1

I could hear music
(sometimes I like it)
out past the wind mill
milling the wind

viva ! the sand dunes
viva ! the breakers
viva ! the swimmers
viva ! their time.

Both of them naked
out in the water
hogging a landscape
entwined in their arms

hugging and kissing
they were dreaming new bedrooms
they were dreaming new houses
they were dreaming new lives

fierce concertos
and busy sonatas
Oh! the sonatas
that sang in my head

2

slowly so slowly
in ascending order
rose from the runway
like whales of the sky

impossible giants
in faun desert dresses
banked and they flew
side on to the beach.

routine manoeuvres
drowned out the piano
the music was gone
the bombers held sway

afterwards silence
and putting their clothes on
touching but barely
they lay on the sand

aftershock falling
they fell into Findhorn
they fell without knowing
they fell like the rain

who gave the order
on a Monday afternoon
to rattle the pebbles
and vindicate love.

Boxers

(Bryony's picture aged 6)

she drew two men fighting
there were no ropes or ring

just boxers on a flat earth
beneath a urchin shaped sun

their shorts bright opposing colours
gloves as big as heads

one had a black eye the other bleeding
they were not perfect

but she knew that the sky was a blue line
at the top of the page

she knew the earth was green
under foot

and she knew even then
that they were in pain

because while they fought
they cried

the tears of both men
flying up into the sky

in
    long
          blue
              dotted
                    lines…

Big Girl Little Girl

Big girl stands by the bar
well within herself
orders a confident cappuccino.

Little girl stands at her hip
rocking and gawking
singing herself.

Big girl is well proportioned
no effort is involved
big girl is really a woman
but she won't forget her roots.

Little girl has long
beautiful hair
which has been lovingly brushed
by big girl.

Big girl smiles
little girl smiles
the whole room smiles
even the chrome handles
on the doors.

It
(for Bryony)

We had been waiting for weeks for it to come
and over pancakes: or was it porridge
one Sunday it announced its imminent arrival.
So we went off to where it would appear
about 5 hours later it came to meet us
out from its difficult journey
where it felt distress
and had been made to eat something nasty.

The moment came: it inflated itself
as though somehow it were collapsible inside
it was not really taking the air at first
which made the welcoming party rush about
with all manner of tubes and scissors
anyway it decided to breathe
and where there was only one
suddenly there were two.

This was quite unfathomable at first
it was very small and beautiful
but had to stay in a plastic see-through box
when I put my hand in to stroke it
something incredible happened
it became her: became love
I became something new
something better
(wasn't expecting that).

Daze of a Week

Moonday

no sleep: tonight we shine: Celine is coming: the lunatics are coming: anything can happen: once she has stripped: *oh heavens…*

Tuneday

is for listening: to the music of cars: the rhythm of fridges: the relaxing tick of grandfathers: the birds will bring banjos and boxes…

Weddingsday

all churches will be like cathedrals: all photographers work for you: (don't feel you have to: many people co-habit happily for years…)

Thirstday

its always hot (or is: in memory) and the beer flows: perhaps we all love: perhaps it is the beer: lets meet up later at the Hoppity Jug…

Fry-upday

the smell of tomatoes chattering in the pan: dispensations today for grumpiness and crying during bad movies…

Saturnday

all hail the gas giant: its rings: its mystery: we have time: we have elbows…

Sun-day

light: fill up the house: light: fill up my mind: light: for the flowers: to see to read: to make pancakes with truly transcendental syrup…

The Monkey Whisperer

I want you to ask him what is wrong
why he is off his bananas
why he rocks back and forth all day long

whisper in his ear
listen to his tiny heart
ask him what it is we have done

(as if we didn't know).

Belly of a Dog

Here I am in the belly of a dog
alongside the raw meat
and shards of bone.

Spitting out hairs
decomposing
while moved along his gut
waiting to be smeared
on the shoe of the world.

Becoming tight
sleek
stinking
acidic
pernicious.

Here I am in the belly of a dog
I fed him good
the recommended diet
but it wasn't enough.

He craved real meat
ate me whole
seemed easier not to fight
his teeth tore my arm
otherwise I'm fine.

It's only a scratch
I forgive him his nature
spared the whip
stroked him away
he sniffed at my weakness.

Here I am in the belly of a dog
if I listen very hard
I can hear panting
and the internal doings
of the shit machine
as it begins to work.

Moth

They eat the flowers, my children, and you don't even notice. Little
prayers to Ra: your god. My god is pale.
I perch on your hand: *how quaint* you say. Death scented: you can't smell
me. My colours draw you: the idea of me.
Eat me I am rebirth. Was at your fathers deathbed. Flew then, straight to
the cradle.
Stay the other side of the window. Leave your light off. Loom over me:
you never will.
Fear me, for my notions run like woolly bears: searching for somewhere
to pupate.

Bar Shark

Swimming, swimming, swimming. If I stop swimming I firmly believe I will drown. I'll sink down into that deep dark that haunts me. For now, this is not a problem. Swimming is easy. Swimming is what I do and I do it so well. In and out of the clubs and bars, with the tide or against the current, its all the same to me. Over the tables, between the stools, among all the pretty fish. At a distance I circle and watch and wait. There is an art to waiting. I haunt the shoal until I smell that smell. I can smell a pretty fish before I see her. She may be clean, she may be soaked in perfume, but she can't hide that scent. That so subtle signal, that tells me when she is ready to be taken.   Loneliness cast like a shadow across her pointless, gulping face. When she is filled to the gills with need and her drink of choice, when she moves to the edge of the shoal, that's when I strike. A flick of the tail, I'm there. All teeth and trapping, I lose the deadness in my eye. Its that moment, in a conversation, when words do my dirty work. When smiles belie what I really want. Because what I really want is meat. I will do practically anything to get my prey. If you want a nice guy, I will renounce my tribe. If you want mean, I can do that. You want to laugh, I'll swim on my back and roll my eyes into the top of my head. The result will be the same. You see, I know who you are. I've been doing this for a very long time. I'm from those unforgiving seas and they have taught me how to hunt, how to feel the vibrations, and to follow that trail of bubbles to its source. I hate you. I need you. I can tell the hunger in a room, see the hunger in your eyes, the hunger in your soul. Its that same hunger which drives me on, and on, through these dim lit places, swimming these fascinating waters, searching for the next pretty fish, the next silhouette, the next moment to defy the dark. Swimming, swimming, swimming.

Rabbits Never Die

he thought to put two in a leafy field
he thought: *one of each*

every month he thought to come back
to see the offspring: *one of each again*

after a year he thought to count them
233 pairs of bob-tails: one of each

the problem in your world Mr Fibonacci
said a merchant one day

is that your rabbits never die
and they all come in pairs: one of each…

The Slaughterhouse is no place for a Lamb

I shall write you tomorrow
when the sun is up

when I have washed
my stained hands

scrubbed the bone
from under my nails

I'll do it early
before I lose heart.

Patchwork Quilt

starling (*a baby star if you will*) not singing
my mother was one: but only by circumstance

last night as I cleaned my glasses on the quilt you made in 1978
I was reading The Goldfinch: you came to mind

why didn't you run with the rest of us
I thought you would: now I can't find you

look there, gazelles swimming under the water
no, dear, they are dead

the baby stars are singing now: clicking: bubbling: popping
like tiny fumaroles: (*I love it* !)

never considered her internal life
she must have had one

I think she would be glad to know it keeps me warm in winter
sometimes too warm: (*last night I had to throw it off*)

you see my darling, they are the ones
not strong enough to cross the river…

now I wander around this foreign city: where I was born
and look for signs that you were here…

Orphan

They are not here: and yet they are here: all the time: sitting, now, in this empty room. They do not speak but know things about me that you don't know. One of them is wearing a check suit, big glasses and a smoky blue tie. The other; I can't see her very clearly but I can hear the choo-choo of her breathing above the hiss of the oxygen.

The Professor and Me

clink-clink: ice in a whisky glass: the closing of a refrigerator door
radio four: in and out of range: crackling logs

in through the skylight: a million miles an hour: *one day you won't exist*
sleeping bag unzipped: shaky clamber down the ladder

gentle tinkle: firelight and lamp: a book being put down: or was it
a newspaper shadows on the horse brass: the French barometer: the
lacquered shillelagh

I just realised I'm going to die one day': perched on the edge of a stool

*we all die eventually son: but that won't be for a very long time
it's something we all have to live with*

mother in bed: the transistor gently phasing: his unblinking eyes
feet cold: wicker chair creaking as he rose:

I used to read you stories but in this case…: his voice was distant and sad
go back to bed lad – tomorrow is another day

cold rungs: paused at the top: ready to return to the same loft bed
everything is different: over my shoulder he is walking to the kitchen.

Shoemaker-Levy 9

I was cart-wheeling too
lost, aimless, angry

in '94 I was 34 years old
and unhappy – though some said I had it all

flying back and forth every day to the edge of space
to where the air runs out and the vacuum begins

I'd look out - knowing I would cross over soon
but not today - in fact I didn't jump until '96

you and me Levy - we both ended up in fragments
lost in the Roche Zone

we fell - we burned
left scars that were visible to the naked eye.

Walmsleys

Today on the road as I splashed through January's muddy puddles
past its bulging rivers and new-born pot-holes
I heard a clamour in the air
a thousand indecipherable arguments
saw a fractured cloud: a troubled shoal: a splitting in the sky
more geese than I've ever seen
more confused than I've ever seen.

Circling: circling back: above the village: my village
it came to me that these were my ancestors: the Walmsleys
perhaps they were not arguing: perhaps they were lost
perhaps magnetic north no longer existed
perhaps heaven was full and they were outraged
at the loss of their entitlement.

I tried pointing but I didn't know which direction: east or west:
hotter or colder
I'm one of you: I'm a Walmsley: can't you tell? I shouted up
but they were too high
for a while they moved off to the south
but later returned
well I'm here if you want me !
but the swarming Walmsleys continued to wheel
broken and unbroken.

My hands were cold on the handlebars, I was hungry
and I still had a way to go
the Walmsleys, I decided, would have to work it out for
themselves…

Firewalker

my ex' is a fire walker
we are still good friends but

she keeps asking me
to break an arrow and stroll among the coals

it will be good for you – she says
you won't burn your feet

people who have done it say
we're changed forever

I say: *I'll go barefoot in the ashes*
after a night of rain

I say: *I'll roll naked in the snow*
at midnight

she smiles knowingly and says
it's not for everyone

Table

he made me when she left
because she took all the furniture

I am rough and ready

sometimes admired by his friends
who set their minds to peasant ends

he eats from me and I am apt to gain
an occasional stain of coffee or chocolate
shit or shinola

I am fine pitch pine
you can dine on my back

or just put things
to cover the wine glass rings

when the little girl sits I creak
my timbers are antique

rafters from a bread factory
and that's a fact
with my six-inch nails
I lack tact but I do the job
as well as any

marble top
moulded
mundane
mantelpiece aspiring
occasional wood-be

proud
able
I am table

Ghost Orchid

fey pale nun
do you pray

when there is no-one to see
the bleeding out of colour

from your over-elaborate wimple
its complexity hinting at vanity

or has history burdened you
with a strange kind of rigor

Re(current)

Dreamed I sieved the river
with a heavy rusted riddle

found the skeleton of a sturgeon
three watches and a medal

a hair shirt and a hat
a notebook of ideas

several conversations
filled with ire and hesitations

bottles stopped with marbles
full of mud and blood and diamonds

some somersaulting fishes
crying out for *water.*

I kept trawling up the river
for something (I can't remember)

hoped I'd know it when I saw it
because inside me was this feeling

and that is how I woke
filled with emptiness and longing

and this is how I live
searching and never finding.

Inhabitants

A wolf pauses in the old orchard
sniffs the air: remembers the smell of her mate
moves off.

A wasp wanders across the back of my hand
calm voice
could be my mother.

Fishmonger fish
half hid by ice, gaping mouth
eyes known oceans.

Roofless cottage: lodger long gone
sounds recur
a chair creaks: a door moves.

Melting ice in a glass of whiskey
clicking and fusing
his philosophy will ensue.

A bowline
in my dreams I can't get the rabbit
to go down its hole.

Sound Bites

This is the sound of a leather belt being pulled smoothly off through the loops in my trousers: a girl told me once it turned her on.

This is the sound, magnified 100 times, of an Asian ladybird eating one of our home species. The noise is small and crunchy. An apple being eaten. A red spotted one.

This is the sound of a roadside bomb. Radio does not do it justice. Violence compressed at a desk in the studio. And we are far away.

This is the sound of a rope tied to a tree. Creaking under the weight of a thirteen year old girl: raped and hanged. This is the sound of fathers crying and policemen eating lunch.

This is the sound of Dolly Parton singing a song because she feels empowered. Her drawling plaintive crooning set some people's hearts on fire.

This is the sound of my trousers falling down. Hardly a sound at all.

Tongues and Bullets

How did she thrive, on blue roses and dragons, on motto's and daggers, on the wisdom she learned from tongues and bullets. On luck, on what was beneath her skin. Not the tattoos, I mean the blood, her strength, her gift for reinvention.

She had eyes that glowed, eyes that glittered, she had positive thought. She knew that the present could dictate the future, but I don't know if she believed it. She would sit opposite me and play a kazoo, the music was naked…

Her red eye make-up brought to mind poppies and war. Her fingers drew attention – sly glances – her fingers drove some men wild but sometimes she used them to rip her own flesh. Love turned a deaf ear to her conversations – but love came to her fingers like wasps returning to the nest

She was so much more than an idea. Once she said *you look sad* and up until that moment I hadn't known – but I was sad. She knew I wanted to be held - simply because she too wanted to be held. Her art was in knowing things by instinct – this girl was pure voodoo…

So stacked, so edible, so broken. A tree staging alone in a field, secretly yearning for the hum and chatter of the forest. I knew one boy who called her *lake fire* but would not divulge the origin of the term…

She was a girl with boyish charm. She was a woman, a prism, she was the captain of the ship. A doodle in someone's sketchbook. A bare-chested Amazon – fatal – pure Lipizzaner. She was an endless poem, a spit, an isthmus reaching out into the bleak and lonely – she was layers on layers…

And I could have been her father, her brother, her lover – but I was none of these things. In the end she was another human being, a moment, a blossom in a garden. And in that way I loved her, passing her in the world, silently wishing her peace and the tenderness of others…

My Sorrow

My sorrow is for them
Not me
Is for merciless time
Its conveyor belt mentality
My last words to her
I'm sorry I could not be a better son.

My letter to him
Yes I wrote my own father a letter
Found later behind the oxygen machine
Earlier he said: *you shouldn't have done that*
But I knew from the fear in his eyes

Now my sorrow has curdled
Is not feint elegant regret
But pure naked guilt
Is a phantom who visits the small dark hours
It finds me in the daylight too
Interrupts my conversations
Effects my breathing
Speeds my fragile heart

My sorrow is now anger
Turned inwards on me
Sometimes others but less
I am angry at the young for being young
The old for reminding me
And when my lover's mother died
I was angry at her
For the way she treated you in life
Yet still you cry
And I cry with you

The wise man I visit says
I must accept death
I do accept death
What I can't accept is the hurt
What I can't accept is my own cowardice
Mother, father, you were there for me
But I left you alone
Because it hurt
And to my daughter I say
When the time comes
I love you
Do what you can
I'll understand

Swiss Army Knife

All the fish are unhooked now: their scales fall in tiny showers at our feet.
Fish heads and guts: small blade and large: we make love under a waterfall

You dress as a nun: I whittle sticks into small Madonna's for tent-pegs.
String bound parcels can be carried with the hook: *pay attention to the*
signals.

Lashed naked to a tree with hikers nearby: you untie my knots
with the corkscrew: *be vocal* she advises
there's a storm coming.

Put extra holes in your leather belt: with this: the reamer.
Open a can of organic beans: later I chip ice off un-named things
Inch forward: fix your eye-glasses.

Pay attention to the signals: de-cork the wine
she picks squirrel meat from between her teeth.

Removes my splinters: *good grooming is essential for both partners*
last symbol of masculinity: she waves it under my nose.

Unwrapping her package she removes her Swiss Army Sex Toy
includes dildo, butt plug, crop and paddle: she reads from the booklet.

I think of the red handle and the white cross
post- apocalypse we will come into our own: I whimper.

Moon and Moon Descending

Will you sit on my face: he asked.
If we can draw back the curtain: it's a full moon: she replied.

For a languid minute nothing happened
she stood pale at the window looking up: a ghost made flesh.

He lay trying to imagine her thoughts
of distances too big
of a lunar isolation so deep it never ended.

He thought she might cry: for beauty: for mortality
but her smile was wide with love
and a certain something else only she knew
(pity, perhaps desire.)

He had a vision then of the first astronaut
emerging in slow grainy motion
from the belly of his craft.

Slowly skipping towards Tranquillity
reaching up with both hands
like a lover meeting his match.

Back in the moment
bathed in reflected glory: she climbed onto the bed

and as she squatted above him he whispered
let me be born: let me return
to that first moment of existence
the first and last true breath

As she came down to rest
there could be no more words
only sweet and fundamental union.

In that singular moon-lit room
sounds of pleasure echoed forever
far out into the black
and unforgiving multiverse.

Back in 1973

back in 1973
why wouldn't you sleep with me

I borrowed my landlords room
it had a leopard skin bedspread

a shower behind a curtain
Zulu spears on the wall

you weren't impressed at all
I'd bought a condom

from the machine in the Dirty Duck
but I wasn't in luck

and actually Donna
neither were you…

Email to the spammer Ernesto Coates

You keep sending me messages Ernesto, about how I could be better in bed something about staying power with these generic pills you're pushin'.

Is that what you said? I could have some zing in my Johnson as well perhaps?

But Ernesto can you make it a bit longer too and how's about that other holy grail - thickness?

Can you make it thicker Ernesto? Girth is where it's at. You see all those girls with fat rich men? It's not the money Ernesto it's not the fancy black limo's or diamond rings. No! Its coz fat men have fat cocks and girls dig girth Ernesto. So forget your generics get on the hamburgers Ernesto: it's cheaper.

For your information Ernesto I do okay among the lassies (oh), like my man Burns used to do back in the day. You see I got something that beats all your pills and your paraphernalia Ernesto. My home boy Rabbie had it too Ernesto, and if you could bottle it you could retire within a few months on the money you made. What is it?

Where you been at Ernesto? I'm talking about poetry man.

I was in bed with some Dutch babe the other night: read her some Lorca (he's one of them old school poets Ernesto). It was his poem about the barren orange tree. This poem, man, its full of duende, you know, a bit of sadness, a bit of yearning but all kind of beautiful - girls got wet for it.

After that she was a sure thing Ernesto

She quite liked the girth too....that girl fell asleep with a smile on her face Ernesto.

She knew what Frederico knew:

'and the night copies me in all its stars' blew her away man.

That's all I had to do – worked like a charm,

food for thought Ernesto,

food for thought…

Wankers

between a man and a woman

(when I first met you)

all conversations are inclined by instinct

(then when I loved you)

to swim to conclusion

(I wanted to know more)

in some mysterious Sargasso

talking and stalking: dancing around the fire

the truth lurks in the shadows

what do men want she said

to build empires the likes of which...

closer and closer

what do women want he said

little circles she whispered.

Discussing Cock-Cages before Work

Domina 1.
mine gets out once a day
a couple of scratches with my long nails
up towards the head and he spills

Domina 2
that's very generous of you
mine gets out once a week
and all it takes is a couple of hot breaths

Domina 3.
mine is only allowed out once a month
one snap of my garter belt and that's him…

…of course I make him lick it all up after

Domina 1.
naturally

Domina 2.
goes without saying

The last thing I read was...

I do so love – to crack open a bottle - of wine with friends
quiet times - by open fires – misty mountains – and good food
I love to travel – I love to chat – I love deep conversations - the last
thing I read was...

I am not a big fan – of sarcasm or racism – I like a man with brains
– brains are sexy - no tattoos please – I can be loyal – I can be your
best friend – my favourite colour is – I've never heard of - the dark
side of the moon – the last thing I read was...

my best friend – is my horse - so if you don't like to ride...don't
bother to reply - my children live at home – I am only 39 – I am
only 39 – I like to go out - and crack open a few – cinema/theatre/
industrial metal – empty beaches – the last thing I read was...

If you like dogs - I'm the girl for you – I went to Paris - for my
honeymoon – money turns me on – money turns me off –suited and
booted I go to work – so when I come home I wear jeans - I like to
cook - a special meal for friends - when we crack open – the last
thing I read was...

I don't know much - about politics – my mother was Dutch – I don't
go out much - but when I do – I can be – the heart and soul of the
party – my friends think I'm mad – come and join me in my madness
– a knight in shining armour – a loveable rogue – the last thing I read
was...

did you survive the weather – I wanted to chat - but I'm not sure

what that is – I like to crack open - when no-one is looking - my favourite
place is - in your arms - my favourite word is - Lepidoptera – it's a
cracking word - I am an incurable romantic – fancy a coffee sometime
– the last thing I read was…

I am very down to earth – my favourite animal – is a dolphin – I am a
vegetarian who loves to party – my friends think I've cracked – my eyes
are blue – my hair is brown – what doesn't kill you - makes you stronger
– black and white movies - on a Sunday afternoon – the last thing I read
was…

I am a lot of fun – I crack my friends up – I love the rain – I am an old
fashioned girl - I like long walks – beside rushing rivers - no jokers – no
married men – if I sound like your type - drop me a line – I like to go to
concerts – when I look in the mirror - it does not crack – I don't believe in
plastic – the last thing I read was…

I never talk - about my star sign - or what happened in the past – I am
happy and curvy - independently minded – if you show me yours – I'll
show you mine – I need a lot of attention – I am of average height
– moonlight/sunlight/candle-light/hedgehogs – find me in the dark – I have
never done this before – the last thing I read was…

cracked up – cracked – I like to crack open – a bottle of good red – there's
a crack – in the door to my heart - open the door – it'll be cracking good
fun – optimism is my -middle name – cracking up - is no longer my game
– I'm much better now – I love to relax - with a cracked open bottle – I am
looking forward – there is only the future - the last thing I read was…

Waiting for Soup

The Co-op doors opening and closing in a gale
admitting invisible customers.

A tall warehouse on a wharf caught by the sun
dressed in sandstone majesty.

The smell of cow shit through the air-con a memory
high up in the back of the nose.

An older lady driving at funereal pace
with a cortege of white vans.

A school boy with a real leather satchel walks home
over a darkly sleeping policeman.

A man on a sponsored sleep-out with the alkies
waiting for soup.

We Slip

you are younger
I am older
I grow timid you
grow bolder
I think of the finish
you have barely passed
the start

I am buried in air like Odhran
(who was buried alive)
not for art but for faith
he jumped willingly
into the hole
but most of us
we slip.

The Windhouse
(Yell, Shetland - said to be the most haunted house in Britain)

come inside its cold

wind song: human human hum

to decline - to go down hill - to slump

there's a conversation and you really have to listen
for an unbidden creak
of a sill or a beam
or the constant dripping or the dissonant breathing
the windhouse is having a conversation
you really have to listen
this is how it goes…

let me in – let me in

louder - quieter - always there

let me in – let me in

birds and hearts (and fear)

the roof gapes: something flutters
wood is no good in the windhouse

entropy: heaven wants them

horse hair plaster: bare laths
order to disorder: mould: organic decoration
the march of a stain

encroaching upon
a pointless flyblown dado

dead white: thighbones

abandoned bedroom
mouldy-sack-was-a-mattress: bird shit blooms
see a girl undressing: mysterious youth

curtseys on the landing
spins three times
and disappears

death of the flesh: death of the illusion of flesh

and finding a broken mirror in a broken bath

welcome stranger

on the doorstep three skulls
sheep: rattling teeth: black-hole eyes

bone china bones

history: family portraits
blurred: eaten
an ossified tea cup
long-time-lost-for-a-saucer
or that delicate sound
or the neat crook of a pinkie

stepping: stepping: the glamour of possibility

a chicken claw shrivelled
hanging from a kitchen shelf
a ghost dog: panting

we will never know: perhaps that's it

walk through walls: down the hall: nights aimless revenant
dominoes and a ribcage
arranged in a back room
slack: slacker...

echo-stones: clouds: moss

glassless casement
fissures and pits on the grey stone: ingress
lichen like a canker: an enchanting pattern
mortar: less now
rain water: damp the killer
damp the life giver
ingress...
ingress...

love: the ephemeral flower

a spray of finger bones: rusty metal springs: a ring
must...

returning

dust: blown away: away

in sight of the plain

built of the rock on which it sits
above the road
in plain sight

a monument to all who pass

all who pass this way
all who have passed
a blade of grass

dead white: thighbones

stories whispered
something buried
lying beneath
the kitchen window

let me in – let me in – let me in…

hidden bones

pale thighs
freckles in the summer…

berries: red hair

endless gales in winter
perfect union by the fire
heiress: shepherdess in winter
goddess for a summer
reborn: in a daughter's eye
in her daughter's eye
in her daughter's eye

goodbye stranger

glances back up the hill
when they left
for the last time
the final drum of a key in a lock
tears accompanied by rain

slipping: sinking: surrender

storm-hurt-vermin-cursed
ceaseless elemental worry
these dark and faded hours
ingress: ingress...

callers

finally they come
but only on long days
as though visiting a grave
quiet and respectful
for some obscure anniversary

drawn: fearful of the bones
hoping to hear laughter from the parlour
or the ticking of a non-existent grandfather

short days: long nights

mostly no-one comes
mostly the sky sees… nothing

wire: choir: desire: rain

the high harmonic strain
of pylon string
strung
from the hip of the hill

a tonal song

falling …

rising …

slicing …

haunting: running: hearing

and when you've come away
when you wake in the dark
when you stop to listen
when you're not too busy
what is it you hear
louder - quieter - always there

let me in – let me in – let me in…

Absence of God

(St Nickolas church, Monnington)

I come here now?

I came before
as a little boy to this
sturdy-oaken-arch of a door.

To this small country church
on a hill where they still
hide the key in the gutter.

The old lock complains
but admits this secular soul.

I walk these boards
smell that waterlogged wood
stand in the pulpit
where preachers and sons of preachers
have spoken and spat their scripture.

Its not trespass
but I know in my bones
that I do not belong.

I push the pedal that pumps the air
pull out a stop and press a key.
The harmonium wheezes like lung diseases
and produces
a single declamatory drone
solo – vibrato.

as a kid it reminded me of horror movies
the dark archetype waiting in the shadows

I keep my finger on the key
its low-mono-tone

travels into the musty air
through my body
outwards
through the pews
the musty hymnals
and the pale marble font...

mmmmmmmmmmmmmm!

Subliminal like a choir humming
carrying out
through the walls of the church
across this quiet green valley
and on in all directions
eventually
to be drowned out
in a crashing and turbulent world.

The falling man, is that a sign?
Or fountains of burning oil

and the smog I saw
over the city
and the hundred mile winds?

What about the children that fly into pieces
in the shopping malls and cities?
Is that a sign?
And the heat and the drought?
And the earthquakes and tsunami?

They bought me here when I was a kid
it was God's house - they said.

Its as though it were yesterday
but they're not here now...

I lift my finger from the key
expecting silence
craving peace

from this insistent gothic vibration…

mmmmmmmmmmmmmm…

But the drone continues:
part of me wants to remain:
part of me wants to run.

I look up
a wasp has come in through a crack
in the stained glass
through the eye of a saint
its long legs hanging
its fearful wings making that sound
as it helicopter-gunships
past cobalt robes and golden haloes.

Towards me he comes
God's custodian in a black and yellow jumper.

Now I am that boy
leaving again
spooked - terrified by a noise
moving in the air

Dragging on the Romanesque door
pulling it open
I'm running away.

Mummy

yes son

you said this is God's house

yes son

why is he never home?